E

BLACK
SEA

ADRIATIC
SEA

YRRHENIAN
SEA

AEGEAN
SEA

IONIAN
SEA

MEDITERRANEAN SEA

ORANI

MY FATHER'S VILLAGE

CLAIRE A. NIVOLA

FRANCES FOSTER BOOKS

Farrar Straus Giroux

New York

For my Sardinian cousins:

FAMILY OF ZIU (UNCLE) PEPPE NIVOLA
Titina, Antonio, Gonario, Giovanna, Donato, Nicola

FAMILY OF ZIA (AUNT) GONARIA NIVOLA SORO
Gesuino, Angelina, Umberto

FAMILY OF ZIU ANTONI NIVOLA
Daniele, Chicca, Mario, Salvatore, Gineddu, Nunzio, Giovanna

FAMILY OF ZIA MARIA NIVOLA COSSU
Luigi, Tonina, Taddeo, Giovanna, Chicca, Nicolino, Giuseppe

FAMILY OF ZIA BURICA NIVOLA COSSU
Peppe, Teresa, Taddeo, Giovanna, Chicca, Luisa, Tore

FAMILY OF ZIA PAOLA NIVOLA SILVAS
Giuseppe, Nicola, Gigi, Gonario, Tina, Michelino

FAMILY OF ZIU CHISCHEDDU NIVOLA
Peppe, Daniele, Mena, Rita, Gianni

and most of all for my father,
COSTANTINO NIVOLA

I n a sea of breathtaking blue, where
dolphins leaped and plunged in play, lay
an island. Tucked here and there along the
white-pebbled shores were grottoes hung
with stalactites. Above, on the rugged cliffs,
tiny goats picked their way among the rocks
and thistles and wild scented thyme. The fruit
on the island tasted like the fruit of paradise,
but wild boars roamed the mountains. There
were nettles that stung, scorpions with
poisonous tails, and bandits who stole sheep
and sometimes kidnapped people.

In the very heart of the island, in a valley,
lay the village of Orani, where my father was
born.

Every year or so, my family traveled far across the ocean to Italy.
An overnight boat took us from the mainland to the island's port,
arriving at dawn.

From there we rode inland, past the scrub oaks and red trunks of
the harvested cork trees, past chalky talc cliffs and expanses blackened
by brush fires.

How long it took to get there! Hour after hour we drove under a scorching sun, until suddenly the curving road plunged down into the valley, and the houses, low and dark on either side, held us close.

The car stopped abruptly and relatives appeared from all around.

Cousins took me by the hand and led me through the thick-walled houses and out into the courtyards.

Under a fig tree, beside the laundry, among the chickens, they asked, "What is it like in America?"

"Oh, it's better here," I always answered, making them laugh in disbelief. And off we went to pick warm plums and cool grapes and to sit on the low stone walls of the kitchen gardens, where tiny lizards dozed in the searing sun.

More cousins appeared and we scattered like birds. Our sandals clattering on the paving stones, we flew along the alleys— up to the right,

down sharply to the left,

out into the blazing brightness of a piazza.

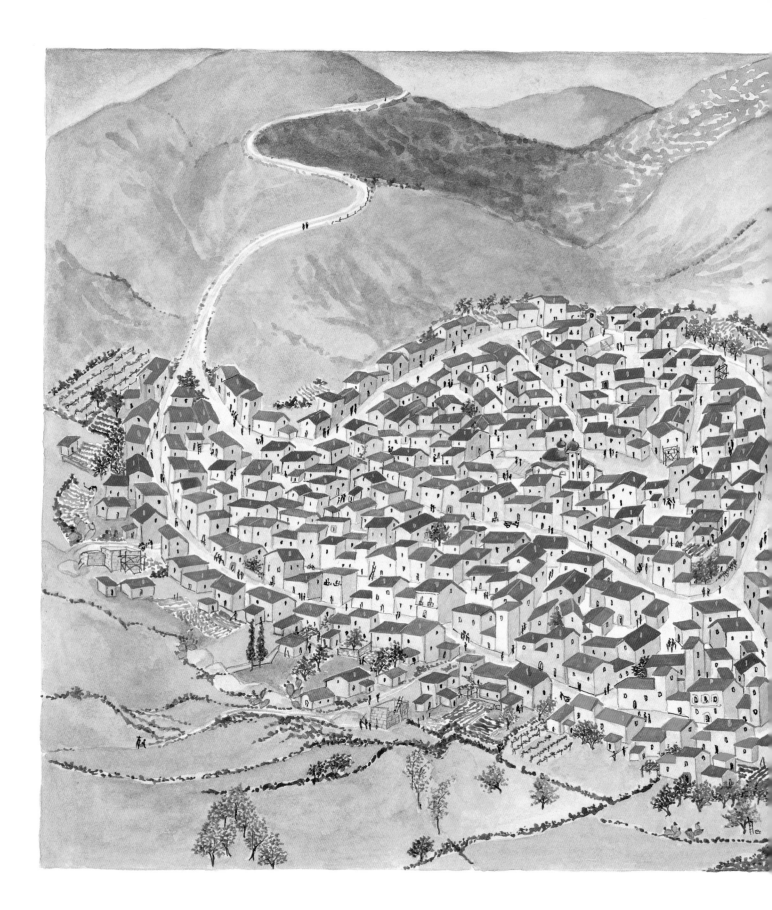

Then back we ran into the cool funnel streets that crossed the
entire sloping village, all the way to the foot of the mountain,

where water sprang from its source, cold and pure.

Like little birds in ever-shifting
combinations, we flew and settled wherever
something was happening, and in Orani,
something was always happening—close
enough to touch.

We ran to see a baby newly born to
a neighbor, to eat ice cream at a café owned
by an uncle,

to ask the miller to grind a bag of wheat into flour, to watch the tailor stitch jackets for the shepherds out of thick velvet—olive green, burnt ochre, brown, and black.

Once, we found a fledgling fallen from its nest and took it to a
cousin who loved birds and had once tamed a hawk.

From courtyards and doorways goats stared at us with their slit pupils, or a tethered donkey twitched flies from its ears.

Old women everywhere offered us holiday biscuits and chocolates. The roadside trees bent low to hand us their fruit.

All the village, it seemed, was ours.

We paused to eat around tables covered with a simple cotton cloth,
in kitchens filled with aunts, uncles, and cousins, all speaking at once.

The cheese came from someone's cow, the honey from someone's
bees. And there were flies, always flies!

Each day flowed into the next. High up in a fig tree, dangling
my legs and peeling the sticky fruit still warm in the sun, I might be
asked,

"Have you ever seen a dead man? No?"

And down we climbed into the streets, the open windows so near
we could hear the plates being cleared from the tables inside.

"Up here," a cousin signaled. We climbed the narrow stairs in
silence to a room where women wept in the shadows. There, in the
center, lay an old man in holiday dress, his face rigid and white and
cold with the unspeakable strangeness of death.

On Corpus Christi day there was a race. Horsemen from a faraway village,

it lasted three days and three nights, with plates stacked high for all
the feasting and, at day's end, a circle dance formed, each person
linked arm in arm in a living chain.

On the outskirts of the village to the east lay the cypress-filled cemetery. We passed that way on the long climb to Santu Franciscu, the tiny chapel alone on a mountain, waiting to be unlocked once a year on its name-day festival.

A breeze always blew up there, smoothing the moss-covered boulders, stirring the wildflowers and the mushrooms that sprang up after a rain.

I would look far down below at the village, so small and neat and silent in the distance, and think of all the noise and life it contained.

All I needed to learn and feel and know was down there. Oh, how I loved that village of Orani!

Then, too soon, came the time to leave. I went back "home" to New York City, with its tall buildings and its grid of straight streets.

Everywhere, there were so many people! It seemed strange that not one of them knew Orani. But then, what different world, I wondered, what Orani of their own might they have known before they traveled here?

AUTHOR'S NOTE

As a child, whenever I drew a map of Europe for school my father would lean over my shoulder and urge me to make the island of Sardinia slightly larger. "The teacher will never notice," he would joke. "After all," he would add more seriously, "it marks the very *center* of the Mediterranean!"

My father was born in 1911 in the village of Orani, in the center of that island at the heart of the Mediterranean. One of ten children, two of whom died before the age of nine, he slept in a bed with five siblings, three with their heads at one end, three at the other. They were almost always hungry and poorly dressed, and they were often ill. His father was a mason, and he too worked from a young age in the trade. At fifteen my father left Orani to become an artist's apprentice in the provincial city of Sassari. Far from the tight-knit world of Orani, he was painfully homesick and lonely. Five years later, awarded a scholarship to study art in Monza, he left for the mainland of Italy, where he was to meet my mother. In 1939, under the dual pressure of fascism and anti-Semitism, he and my mother emigrated to America, where my brother and I were born and where my parents lived for the rest of their lives.

The distance my father traveled from Orani to America was enormous—in more than just miles. The pull of Orani never lost its hold on him.

I was four when my father first took us back to his hometown; we were to visit frequently throughout my childhood. There were still no bathrooms in the houses then, and the gutters in the center of the cobbled streets flowed with more than just water. But this was already the 1950s, Europe was recovering after the devastation of the Second World War, and times were better, much better for Orani than they had been when my father was growing up. New houses were being built—many of them by my mason cousins and uncles—spreading the village outward from the old center. Old houses, with their uneven stucco walls, were being abandoned; the new houses had big rooms, marble floors, *and* bathrooms! Often there was no running water for many hours of the day, but the bathrooms were built to rival those of Hollywood stars, with lightbulbs framing the mirrors.

Cars were still a rarity, and the life of the community, as it always had, unfolded largely in the streets. Old men sat on benches; women and girls ran errands with jugs or broad baskets balanced on their heads, greeting neighbors with *"giorno"* if it was before noon, and *"sera"* if it was after. Men still rode donkeys, and once a horseman—*"un bandito,"* my cousins whispered—rode clattering through a narrow street as we jumped into a doorway, hearts in our throats, to make way for him. At dawn, shepherds led their sheep through the village to pasture, a cloud of tinkling bells. At dusk, the swallows swooped from their nests under the house eaves, crisscrossing the settling darkness. The village was a bowl formed by the mountains all around, with the sunlit or star-filled sky as its lid.

Orani was a complete world and just the right scale for a child. Everything happened there—all the tragedies and joys—but they happened in a contained place, among family and neighbors, where everyone knew and cared, so that as a child I could comprehend and feel that each part fit into life's whole. It was there that I saw where the things I ate came from—the tree, the plant, the animal—and how each food was made by the work of someone's hands. In Orani, I felt at the literal source of everything, and how thrilling that was!

I continue to go back to Orani. My cousins and I are older, and the village too has grown up. That moment has passed—when I was a child; when Orani was shaking free of abject poverty, yet no one had too much; when new ways had not yet torn it away from what was rich in its past. Now there are televisions and computers luring people indoors. Cars park in, or race through, streets meant for people and donkeys. Street life, the pulse and glue of a village, is all but gone. Relatives, though they may live a stone's throw apart, rarely visit one another.

The world is always changing. That little world too, which I have tried to paint for you in all its immediacy, continues to change. And yet each time I go back, I feel again that charge, something more real and alive than I experience in any other place. Human contact is immediate, warm, and intense. We are in a valley. The sky is overhead, and around us the gentle mountains. I am once again at life's center!